Imagination's Reverie

"Dancing in the dark, to end of love,
we are the unfinished song
forever alive in the shadows of time."

— Candice James

(excerpt from Dancing in the Dark pg 29)

Also by Candice James

Spiritual Whispers (Silver Bow Publisghing) 2023
Atmospheres *(Silver Bow Publishing)* 2023
The Depth of the Dance *(Silver Bow Publishing)* 2023
Behind the One-Way Mirror *(Silver Bow Publishing)* 2022
The Call of the Crow *(Silver Bow Publishing)* 2021
The Path of Loneliness *(Inanna Publications)* 2020
Rithimus Aeternam *(Silver Bow Publishing)* 2019
Haiku Paintings *(Silver Bow Publishing)* 2019
The 13th Cusp *(Silver Bow Publishing)* 2018
Fhaze-ing *(Silver Bow Publishing)* 2018
The Water Poems   *(Ekstasis Editions)* 2017
Short Shots   *(Silver Bow Publishing)* 2016
City of Dreams   *(Silver Bow Publishing)* 2016
Merging Dimensions   *(Ekstasis Editions)* 2015
Colors of India   *(Xpress Publications India)* 2015
Purple Haze   *(Libros Libertad)* 2014
A Silence of Echoes   *(Silver Bow Publishing)* 2014
Shorelines   *(Silver Bow Publishing*) 2013
Ekphrasticism   *(Silver Bow Publishing)* 2013
Midnight Embers   *(Libros Libertad)* 2012
Bridges and Clouds   *(Silver Bow Publishing)* 2011
Inner Heart, a Journey   *(Silver Bow Publishing*) 2010
A Split in the Water   *(Fiddlehead Poetry Books)* 1979

Imagination's *Reverie*

by

Candice James

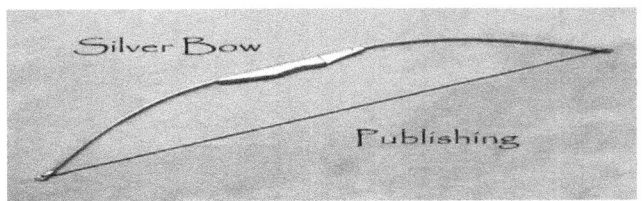

Box 5 – 720 – 6th Street,
New Westminster, BC
V3C 3C5   CANADA

Title: Imagination's Reverie
Author: Candice James
Copyright © 2023 Silver Bow Publishing
Cover Painting: "Nevada Night Oasis "Candice James
Layout/Design: Candice James
ISBN: 9781774032695 (print)
ISBN: 9781774032701 (ebk)j

All rights reserved including the right to reproduce or translate this book or any portions thereof, in any form except for the use of short passages for review purposes, no part of this book may be reproduced, in part or in whole, or transmitted in any form or by any means, electronically or mechanically, including photocopying, recording, or any information or storage retrieval system without prior permission in writing from the publisher or a license from the Canadian Copyright Collective Agency (Access Copyright)

Library and Archives Canada Cataloguing in Publication

Title: Imagination's reverie / by Candice James.
Names: James, Candice, 1948- author.
Description: Poems.
Identifiers: Canadiana (print) 20230470416 | Canadiana (ebook) 20230470424 | ISBN 9781774032695
   (softcover) | ISBN 9781774032701 (Kindle)
Classification: LCC PS8569.A429 I43 2023 | DDC C811/.54—dc23

Email: info@silverbowpublishing.com
Website: www.silverbowpublishing.com

Imagination's Reverie

To all the dreamers
who dare to dream
imagination's fantasies.

Imagination's Reverie

FOREWORD

There are many types of love: of the flesh, of the heart, of the mind, of the spirit, AND esoteric, ethereal, surreal and fantasy This book expresses love in all facets and measures: real and imagined

Love is love is love is love in all forms on earth as it is in heaven.

Imagination's Reverie

Contents

Inspiration / 11
I Who Was Dead / 12
Take My Breath Away / 13
Never Strangers / 14
Too Beautiful / 15
The Deep / 16
The Dance Floor Of Dreams / 17
Your Presence / 18
That Kind Of Day / 19
Even Before I Heard Your Voice / 20
Imagination's Reverie / 21
Such A Sweet Dream / 22
The Threads Of Your Essence / 23
These Moments / 24
The Music Plays / 25
When I Lay Down To Sleep / 26
I'll Lay You Down In My Love / 27
Somewhere / 28
Dancing In The Dark / 29
In The Sweet Spot / 30
Limitless Slumber / 31
Perfect / 32
Degrees Of Depth / 33
The Dream / 34
Breathless / 35
Vessels / 36
Unnoticed Intervals / 37
The Thought Of You / 38
Doves And Angels / 39
The Distant Silence Of Your Absence / 40
Missing You / 41
The Whisper Of Your Voice / 42
This Night Without You / 43
Creation / 44
Desire / 45
The Combination / 46
That One Drop Of Water / 47
Thought / 48

Faint Whispers In The Night / 49
Flirting / 50
The Air I Breathe / 51
Polestar / 52
Message / 53
You Are / 54
All That Is You / 55
Timing Is Everything / 56
Hazy Line / 57
I Close My Eyes / 58
Moments In Life / 59
I Thank You / 60
Evidence / 61
Imagination / 62
A 24 Karat Gold Embossed Day / 63
Caught In This Web / 64
Love's Misty Ghost / 65
Perfection Personified / 66
The Only One I See / 67
I Will / 68
I Get By / 69
The Longing / 70
I Adore You / 71
Entranced / 72
If Wishes Were Songs / 73
Last Night / 74
In My Mind / 75
The Wait / 76
Fantasy's Salve / 77
There Will Come A Time / 78
And Even Then / 79
Even Deeper / 80
Higher / 81
Longer Than Forever / 82
Shine This Dream / 83
YOU / 84
Your Rhythm / 85
YOU Forever / 86
We Have No Choice / 87
Author Profile / 89

Inspiration

When it arrives
    the creative craving is sated
        as the feelings and words
        tumble down
        in embers and flames
        onto the papers of timeless time
    where fantasy and imagination reside
      in the warm hold of the soul.

The first time I saw you,
    I recognized you immediately
        from some hazy forgotten past
        that wasn't completely forgotten.

        And there you were ...
        standing tall,
        my inspiration.

In my passion
and my fashion,
my tender innermost fashion,
I have always loved
the idea of being in love
and I have always loved you
my imaginary, fantasy lover..

I Who Was Dead

I see your face
and your smile.

And I who was dead
am alive again
as I melt in the glow of your eyes.

Have I ever told you
when I see your face
or hear your voice
the world becomes a love song?

It's true.

And when I touch your hand ...
I, who was dead,
am suddenly alive again.

Take My Breath Away

Some night
        we'll dance in the devil's cabaret.
I'll take off my mask
        and shed my disguise
                and my heart
                        will fall at your feet.

I'll barter my heart to live in your love
and ride high in the tidal rise of your eyes.

I'll surrender my soul in sweet crucifixion
to die in the echo of your heartbeat.

        Even now, slowly...
slowly I'm ebbing into your soul.

        Take my breath...
        take my breath away.

Never Strangers

In the expanse of an all-pervading silence
      I still hear your voice:
           soft; gentle.

In the thick mist of a blinding fog
      I still see your fabulous face:
           your eyes smiling.

      Never strangers
      I knew your eyes and soul.
           the moment I saw your face
         and heard your voice.

Too Beautiful

Deep in the clutch of sleep and dreams:
I pull out a beat from your heart.
      It glows crimson
         in the dark of my night
              and lights the pathway
                  that leads to us.

I hold the beat I took from your heart
      in the pulsating palm of my hand.
         It dissolves through my flesh
            into my being
         and plays the music you are.

      I try to categorize it
            but it's too beautiful.

            And you ...

           you are
           too beautiful for me.

The Deep

As I drift into sleep
and the deep of my dream,
    we lay beneath
a slow moving, benevolent sky
    suspended above
  a moonlit sapphire lake.

    We are
    the lovers
  sinking into love's lake
stilling the earth and everything in it,
in the crush of our human explosion

  In the deep of my dream
    we become...
      real.

The Dance Floor Of Dreams

I recognize this new music
I've heard so many times before.
      There's a groove to the beat
      and a remembered heat
that opens wide the yearning in me.

      Suddenly I see you.
  I know this living dream so well.

   There's a look in your eyes
that melts my heart and sears my soul.

    In the tight of your embrace
    at the dark end of the room
      I fall in love again
      remembering when
        we were not strangers,
       when we danced
   on the dancefloor of dreams
        so close
   passing through each other.

       Another time.
      Another place.

    Forever in my heart.

Your Presence

I scan the room
>off and on,
>eyes flickering
>fore and back.

>Hoping you might be
somewhere in the room.
>Hoping I might be
somewhere in your heart.

Time passes.
>Everything is dull, hazy.
>The music is nondescript.

>THEN SUDDENLY
>>YOU
>walk in the room.

The music takes on a new high.
The night transmutes from brass to gold.

I lay myself down in the glow of your essence
>>and come alive
>inside the atmosphere
>your mere presence creates.

That Kind Of Day

It's that kind of day.
    Inspired.
       Wrapped in spirit feathers.
           Soft to the touch
                before it dissolves.

At the edge of my vision
    you approach
        on wing and a sigh;
    and I think I hear angels singing.

    Music for the lost and lonely.
    Eye candy for the weary soul.
    A map for the lost sojourner.
    And a familiar song for me.

        It's that kind of day.
   One that promises bright stars at night,
      an enchanted evening,
        a love song ...
   and passionate dreams
      of you and i.

Even Before I Heard Your Voice

A bolt from the blue
    And I was
Ablaze and wanting
    From the lightning strike
        I never saw coming.

    Distracted by the music
        Blasting through my mind
    I never heard the warning bells ringing.
        I never saw you coming

    Then suddenly
    your face was all I saw.

Your eyes held me:
        Mesmerized.
        Hypnotized.
        Paralyzed.

    I was yours ...
even before I heard your voice.

Imagination's Reverie

So soft, this blanket of make believe.
So beautiful, this everlasting moment.

    As I swim through
the waters of timeless time.
    I become
                    a word
                    a rhyme
                    a poem
                    a song.

          AND...

when I'm lost in these moments
of imagination's sweet reverie,
you are the only music I hear.
your face is the only face I see.

        YOU are ...
                my reverie.

Such A Sweet Dream

I'm in love with the idea
of being in love with you:

>Such a sweet escape,
>Such a sweet dream.

I'm warmed by the thought
   of laying with you:

>Such an excitement.
>Such a contentment.

I'm in love with the idea
of being in love with you.

>Such a sweet release.

>Such a sweet. sweet dream.

The Threads of Your Essence

In my dreams I fade into
the diamond dusted trail
I see you walking down
trying to grasp the threads
      of your essence
and press them to my breast.

      Solid...
   then hazy

      hazy...
   then gone.

Sleep ebbs away,
   and so do you

I will press the threads
  of your essence
    to my breast

      until
  the dream returns.

These Moments

There are moments
I've fallen in love with:
that coil around my heartstrings
and turn me inside out,
into the song I used to be,
singing my body electric
and setting my soul on fire.

        These are the moments
          of paradise lost
       that are never truly lost;
        that live and breathe
      with a life of their own ...
past, present and future.

Whenever I'm lost to the world,
   lost in these moments
  of a sweet imagination's
     total surrender,

     you are there too.

The Music Plays

The gleam in your eyes.
The gentle nod of you head
toward the dance floor.

      The music plays
        is inviting
     and so are your arms.

I feel your body pressing into mine.
     The hot, cool heat
draws me into   the beat of your heart.

      And I am captured
     in the tight of desire
       so tight
    I can almost taste it.

  Ablaze
in the deep of the moment
  I graze the depth
  of your passion.

      I am captured
     in the tight of desire
    and hungry for the dream
     I see in your eyes.

    And the music plays...

    The music plays.

When I Lay Down to Sleep

When I lay down to sleep at night
thoughts of you edge into my mind.
      I wonder if you are sleeping.
      If you're dreaming.

      I fancy you are dancing
         in your dreams
         with me.

      Then I see us
      laying down
on the satin sheets of the dream
in the aftermath of the dance.

When I lay down to sleep
      I move into the tender night
        moving toward
      where your dream resides,
that I can blend mine into yours
      and spend forever
        with you.

I hear you whispering my name softly
      and the glow of your eyes
      is the last thing I see
      as I fall asleep.

I'll Lay You Down In My Love

I will be your music.
I will be your candle in the wind,
your primordial spark.

I will be your water,
I will be your breath.
I will be your fire.

When you lose yourself,
I will always find you.

I'll lay you down in my love
and keep you warm forever.

Somewhere

I'm dreaming I'm awake
   and
    it's raining
somewhere in the world.
    but not here.
I see only soft sunshine
reflecting in your eyes.

    It's snowing
somewhere in the world,
    but not here.
It's too hot beside your heart
for snow to manifest
much less survive.

The weather is inclement
somewhere in the world,
 but never in my world
 when you are near me.

Dancing in the Dark

In my dreams
even when your image is hazy
and unrecognizable
I still know it's you
because I feel you
on every level of existence.

The depth of passion
I see in your eyes
attracts me like no other lover.

In the ebb and flow
of falling asleep
I drift on invisible waves,
into the ebony night sky
travelling toward you.

Closer and closer;

I swear I feel your breath on mine.
The atmosphere becomes electric.

Dancing in the dark,
to end of love,
we are the unfinished song
forever alive
in the shadows of time.

In the Sweet Spot

One of my sweetest daydreams:
Your glistening body lowers onto
      the mattress.

    I crumble and sigh
  and I slide into your arms
    your mouth, your body
      and your soul.

It feels so surreal and yet so real.

    Inherently ever present in my every cell
      you run rampant, savagely,
        silently, soothingly
        through this heart
    you're so much a part of,
    so deeply entrenched in.

  In the sweet spot
of my sweetest daydream,
    I am yours, always,
        and
    you belong to me.

Limitless Slumber

If I do not lie next to you now
in this winter season of our lives
and if I do not rest next to you
in this lifetime,

I will
In the endless days and nights
of our limitless slumber.

I will.

That Secret Space

Take me to your heart
and hold me closer
with every beat
so I can really feel it.

Let me ride the tidal rise
I see deep in your eyes.

    But, most of all,
take me to that secret space
   in your beautiful soul
    that I may abide
in the deep of your love
      forevermore ...

and I will give every part of me
        to you
in sweet and total surrender.

Degrees Of Depth

I wait
while a lonely violin
plays softly in the shadows

YOU approach
and the world is a symphony

The Dream

The dream
flames through my thoughts.
My speech grows thick.

You
slip into my bed
sighing softly.

Consciousness calls...

The dream
has slipped away again
leaving only
a dying ember
on the damp of my breast
and the taste of you
still wet on my lips.

Breathless

Stripped down to the bone
in the naked gaze of passion
    I melt into the flame
      in your eyes

        In the sweet of the wet
        and the wet of the sweet
        I bleed
        through the needle's eye
        of need
        in the sweetest
        of sweet surrenders

And I am...

Breathless.

Vessels

A double shot of Southern Comfort
and a glass of Balvanie Scotch

> Both on the rocks ...
> but not the crave.

A man and a woman
  melting together
on a mattress of sultry dreams.

> Outside the weather
> is undecided.

> Inside the mood
> is wired with desire.

> Human vessels
> in their element

> electrify!

Unnoticed Intervals

On a subconscious level
  I think of you

In the space between seconds,
the gap between pulse beats
    I think of you
even in those unnoticed intervals.

Right from the first time I saw you
     you have been
    always on my mind,
    forever in my heart,
    etched into my soul …

        and …
  I know not why …

  I know not why.

The Thought Of You

      The thought of you
    seductively entrancing
        softly pulls me
into wanton and lurid daydreams
     and anticipated desires
      that occupy my mind
     and set me to craving
       your nearness,
        your touch,
           you.

Doves and Angels

I will awaken the doves
that lay sleeping on this page
        and walk across the burning embers
            of yesterday
to taste the sweet of your flesh
and bathe in the blood of your heart.

A ring of angels will form overhead
and witness the burning of my soul
            for you;
and the crimson staining of my heart
            for you.

 I will etch your name
            into the quick of the river ...
       the river I have created
           for you
         from the core
       of my deepest craving
        and the depth
      of my carnal need.

   Then
       you will come to me
            and the doves and angels
                will sing in unison again.

Imagination's Reverie

The Distant Silence Of Your Absence

In miles, kilometers
decibels or tones
I don't like distance
   or silence
  separating us.

Although, really, in essence,
     near or far,
   vocal or muted
there is no separation
   in this fantasy.

  Knowing this
makes the distance
   the silence
  the exhaustion
   bearable.

So I'll just keep writing
and trying to get you back
   into my dreams
     in this
    the fallout
of your absence.

This full effulgence
of the distant silence

  of your absence.

Missing You

The atmosphere
in this daydream
 is thin yet hazy
wrapped in a shawl
   of longing.

The invisible doorway
      is hollow.
     The chair
I visualize you sitting on ...
       empty.

       And
  so is my daydream ...

Full of emptiness;
 trying to find you
my imagination is weary
       and
     missing you.

The Whisper Of Your Voice

Your eyes and your touch
pull me into their magic
and the whisper of your voice
tugs at my heart
caresses my spirit
and warms my soul to the bone.

Thirst slaked
and appetite sated,
still,
I hunger

for more of you.

This Night Without You

    An empty feeling
inside a smile turned upside down.

    A wet dream
inside an invisible tear,

        This night
        without you in it
          is cold

and I'm stoned to the bone
      with the blues
    in the middle of
      a jazz song
that makes me want you
        even more
in the middle of this night
      without you

      in my dream..

Creation

I am creating
A space in place and time
    for you and I.

In this space
    we will lay
    on a sundrenched
    whiskey slaked beach
    of our making.

We will move slowly into
    a moon-kissed night
    to lay each other down
    on a blanket of dreams
        in the deep southern comfort
        of each other.

And we will re-dream the dream we are,
    have always been,
        will ever be.

I am creating this space
    for you and I only
    that no other may enter.

Desire

There's just something about you.
    that set my soul afire.

    Walking a high wire
      in my mind
        I falter.
        then fall
into the deep of your soul.

        You rock me gently
        in the cradle of your love
        and I am aflame
        in desire's court
        as I burn for sooth
          in your gaze..

The Combination

Faces have
      Implied windows and doors;
         locks and keys.

Feelings have emotions and secrets;
      safes with combinations.

         I'm trying to find the key
            to your dream.
        because I believe
           you have
         the combination
           to mine.

That One Drop Of Water

Soft, warm summer rain
        on my face..
A cool breeze
        teasing my hair
        on a hot August night.

   In the winter of my years
you are a ray of blazing sunshine
    lighting up my hazy world,
burning the chaff
        off my worn and weary heart.

               And I am
           that one drop of water
           sent to slake your spirit
           destined to quench your thirst.

Thought

All creation is thought.
Everything begins as a "thought";
then it out-pictures itself
into reality.
        It has no choice.

All thought is energy
and all energy
must become real.
        It has not choice.

I think about you.
You are in my thoughts.
Some have already
out-pictured themselves
into reality.

Some haven't ... yet.

Faint Whispers In The Night

I hear breathing.
      Are you near?
           or am I just dreaming.

    Sometimes its almost too real
        but then
     could it ever be too real?

      No. Impossible.

It's a manifestation
      of a parallel reality
spilling into my dream.

A hunger and a longing
I recognize immediately
    punctuated by
faint whispers in the night;
  soft misty love letters
straight from your heart.

Flirting

There's flirting ...
       and then ...
            there's flirting.

      What I do with you
   falls somewhere
      in between
  but is so much more than ...
    and deeper and hotter:

an imaginary branding iron
    intent
on leaving its mark
   indelibly imprinted
 on your beautiful soul.

    I believe it is spelled
       L-O-V-E

The Air I Breathe

At the end of every rainbow
       I see you standing tall.
At the edge of every teardrop
       I visualize your image.

    When I'm all alone,
    I'm never alone,
there are always thoughts of you.

       At the edge of all my dreams
   I can feel your breath on mine
       I see your face.
     You touch my hand.

     I feel your soft caress
       in all my dreams.

You're slowly becoming
         the air I breathe.

Polestar

I was a ship at sea.
You were the polestar
that led me
back into my harbour
of living words and creativity.

We passed by each other
in a suspended moment in time ...
and then we went back
to our separate places
in time.

Message

The simple message is.
    really ...
        no message at all.

    It tells me all I need to know.
    I can hear, subliminally,
        the timbre.
        the inference.
        the sound.

Even though there is no message
    I recognize all the tonal qualities.
        It's YOU

You Are

You're the flame
that melts the ice.

        You're the ice
        that breaks the fever.

You're the water
that slakes the thirst.

        You are life
        that wakes the dead.

You're the breath
the height, depth and breadth
of all I'll ever need.

        You are
        my desire.

All That Is You

To touch,
to taste,
to drink
      all that is you.

To sleep inside the scent of you.
      Obsession personified.

      Caught up in a shaft
      of times illusion
      and embraced
      by the dream of you
      I linger in the starlight
      warmed by the fires
      of my imagination.

I would trade all my coveted treasures
  to sleep in the dream that is you:
      To touch,
      To taste,
      To drink
            All that is you

Imagination's Reverie

Timing Is Everything

In music and life timing is everything.
In passion and love timing is everything.
Timing can make it Timing can break it.

> The push and pull
> Of hours, minutes and seconds
> The swing and sway
> Of days, week, months.
>
> The push and pull of time
> The swing and sway of love.
>
> And then there is YOU.
> The dream I am dreaming.
>
> It's all so right
> But it's all so wrong.

The feeling is so right
But the timing is wrong
    AND sadly,
timing is everything.

Hazy Line

It's a hazy line
>between love and fancy.
>It blurs the mind
>tempts the heart.

In a fingerprint impression
of full body immersion
and soul-centred emotions
the moments glow
then spark into flame
>in the mind,
>in the heart,
>in the soul.

In so many of my daydreams
>you enter in passion's wake;
>and the feel of the moment
>kindles, catches fire
>and sets me a-sail
on the hazy line between love and fancy
and the incoming tides of sweet surrender
>... again and again.

I Close My Eyes

Sometimes
      I catch a hint of you.
      Your scent in the air near me.
      Almost as if you are here.

      Maybe you are here:
      In essence.
      In ghostly guise,
      In spirit.

Or perhaps it is just a manifestation
      of my desire
      to have you near.

      I close my eyes,
set myself into the magic of dance,
      and melt into
the magnificence of entanglement
      with you.

Moments In Life

Through the rippling mirrors
of life, breath, and death
      I saw you in a moment
      of timeless time.

I whispered your name.
You turned to look at me
before you slipped away
into the next moment of life..

Moments in life:
      So many taken.
      So many missed.
      So many protected.
      So many lost.

We are all just "moments in life"
in the catch and release of destiny,
  travelling the pathways of time.
      Sometimes our paths intersect
          and become one.
      Sometimes they veer off course
          and "our" moment is lost.

And I am left to wonder...
          How many times
          have we lost each other?

I Thank You

The moments I spend in dreams with you
are indelibly imprinted on my memory
and burned into my soul.

     Oh how I love romance.
And oh how you bring it out in me.

I love the idea of love
And I love being in love.

I'm not sure if this
is a blessing or a curse.

I do know I feel more alive
when I am falling in love

       And

 I thank you for
 bringing me alive
     in this
the winter of my life.

Evidence

In the coinage of emotion
and the double-edged arrow of love
despair is the other side of passion.

The arrow plunged into the heart
sparks the embers of passion.
      The heat of the flame
        evidenced by
    the invisible scar on the heart.

The arrow piercing the soul
Flays it open in a torn death.
      The depth of the cut
        evidenced by
    the invisible smear of tears.

.
        Always,
     unseen evidence
    is the most evident
    and sometimes ...
sometimes you may see
  the smears and scars
  of old hurts in my eyes.

Imagination

Paradise,
        once an illusion,
        seems in reach
    when you are near me.

        And then,
I imagine fantasy becoming reality
and I wonder if imagination
is the playground of fools
or the arena of sages.

No matter.
        It is my best friend
        when I think on you.

A 24 Karat Gold Embossed Day

Meeting you has become
a 24-karat gold embossed day
   shining like a diamond
            in my memory.

      The first time I touched you
          I felt the world spin
              in a new way;
      in a sensuous sway
      of gentle electricity.
that climbed into my heart
         and scaled the precipice
        of my being,

      Hot blooded,
you have taken the bite out of winter
         and turned my world to gold
          simply by being ...
            near me.

Imagination's Reverie

Caught In This Web

You are so mesmerizing
        and I am so obsessed.

    Caught in this web
        of uncensored dreams,
        unbridled fantasies
        and coveted illusions
        I would be content to be:

            A droplet of vapour
            in the breath you take.

            A glint of desire
            in your twinkling eyes.

            A wanton thought
            in your beautiful mind.

    Caught in this web
        Of uncensored dreams
        woven with the threads
            of desire for you ...

            I remain
                obsessed.

Love's Misty Ghost

Love's misty ghost
is embedded in my heart
and walks with me down this road I travel
      where pebbles turn to stones
      and stones become mountains
      as I try to find a way to get to you.
To scope out a place in your heart
that I can rest in and lay claim to:

      Where I can paint gorgeous images
      to decorate your beautiful soul.

      Where I can brew a special magic
      to ease my way into your psyche;
      so I can dry your wettest tears
      and erase your deepest scars.

Where love's misty ghost and I
can lay with you forever
inside the deep kiss of love.

Perfection Personified

Total fascination
coupled with infatuation
      has invaded my world.

            Now escalating emotions
            and sweet inspiration
            keep me magnetized to
            daydreams and fantasies
            and
            continual thoughts of you:
            so attractive
            so sexy
            so inimitable.

      Perfection personified!

The Only One I See

When I see you approaching me
everything else becomes
        hazy, blurred, an illusion.
And as you draw nearer I tingle
with excitement   becoming more real
        inside this dream I'm dreaming;
            this dream of you and I.

Nothing can compare to this feeling you arouse in me:
        This emotion without boundaries.
        This complete obsession
    of heart and soul that lives and breathes
    with a will of its own.

            That knows not the words:
                Disbelief.
                Impossible.
                Wrong.
    But knows well the words:
                Desire.
                Need.
                Love.

When you walk into my dream
        the world disappears.

            You're the only one I see.

I Will

I want to be the sun
in the centre of your heart:
To light all the pathways
and illuminate the darkened corners..
To dry all its tears and erase all its scars.
To wipe every hurt away
leaving no trace or remnant
of sorrows you've had to endure.

I want to be the salve for all your wounds:.
    To ease you pain
    To calm your soul.

I want to be the one you come to:

    When you're lonely.
        I will stay with you.
    When you're sad.
        I will ease your sorrow.
    When you're in need of a soft caress.
        I will lay my hands on you.
    When you need to be loved.
        I will love you.

        I will love you.

I Get By

When we part
       my spirit is left simmering
             my soul burning,
                   my heart aching
       and I am left wondering at the fact
that I can endure your absence.

Normal life goes on
       but there is a hard emptiness
             encrusted at the edges
of days and nights
       without you.

I get by and continue on each day
       casually; as usual.
             The only difference now is
thoughts of you invade the hours
       minutes and seconds.

       They comfort
             and they ache.

       When you're not near
      time passes by slowly
             on broken wheels
             and flattened tires..

       I get by ... but, just barely.

The Longing

I whisper your name
as I lay down to sleep
    and beseech
    the keeper of dreams
to let mine come close to yours
    in the heat of passion's breath.

    Just to hear your voice,
    just to feel you near,
    falling asleep in my arms
    in my dream.

    The longing never ends.

I Adore You

Did I ever tell you how good it feels
        to be with you in fantasyland
              and feel your warmth
                      and scent?

        It's true..

All my tomorrows are closing in
        and the walls are falling down
              and I'll see you again,
          `feel you again.

        Even if it is only for a short time,
            it is what I live for.

        Better loved and cherished,
            desired and wanted
                    you'll never be.

        I adore you.

Entranced

Whenever I see you smile
    my world is brighter
and when you look at me
    I am entranced.

    In my daydreams of desire
    I'm creating a sea of love
       to surround us

    I'm building a ship
     that we may sail
    the deepest waters
    of love and emotion
     and each other.

    so i can taste your smile
    and you can feel my desire.

    When you look at me
      I am entranced,

       Always,
      I am yours

If Wishes Were Songs

In the worn crease
of another fading midnight,
      I reach for my guitar
and wish you were here with me.

I imagine you, tonight,
  on the other side of my world;
    so near and yet so far
       and I wonder ...
            if you're sleeping ...
      perhaps dreaming
a sweet dream of you and I.

I close my eyes
      strum my guitar
and hum an old country song
   one of your favourites.

I want to sing you to my side.

   If wishes were songs
  you'd be here with me.

Last Night

I once told you I'd never make you cry
      and I meant it.

But last night, in a parallel dimension
      I asked one too many questions
          and you began to weep
              momentarily.

    Last night when you wept
    I saw your tenderness,
        your sensitive side
        and loved you even more
        than I thought possible.

In My Mind

I close my eyes for a moment
and you are here with me,
        So beautiful.

I open my eyes
        and you are not here.

Everything must be formed
        in the mind
before it can out-picture itself
        into reality.

        So I sit here
forming the future in my mind.

        Imagination is
        the architect of reality.

Soon you will appear.

The Wait

Today I wait
to see my mind image out-pictured.
      To see you coming to me.

Tomorrow
      I will continue to wait again.

And then the next day,
      ad infinitum,
            until you come to me.

Fantasy's Salve

What harm in fantasy
if it soothes the aching heart?

What harm in make-believe
if it eases the weary mind?

What harm in dreaming
if it revitalizes the soul?

      No harm
  in wishing or hoping
    or believing

Imagination is a gift
      and fantasy is its salve.

There Will Come A Time

There will come a time
when you will come to me
      too late.

When you will have the crave
      and the desire
           for me.

When you will want to be in my dreams.
      When you will pine for me
           like you have pined
              for no other.

That will be the time
      you will seek out
           fantasy's salve.

  ... There will come a time.

And Even Then

You are the deep end of the ocean
and I long to dive into you
        and never resurface again.

I want to feel your exquisite wet
bringing my body and soul
to a fever pitch high
on your swift-shot current
that will imprison me
in your water world of love
and hot secrets forever.

        And even then,
forever will not be long enough.

Even Deeper

I want to live in your kiss
   and be your breath.
I want to flow through your being
   and know every part of you.

I want to touch every part of your body
and memorize it onto my fingertips
    to imprint it into my soul
     as braille for the heart;
    the entirety of my desire
     that I may feel you
       even deeper
than the depth of the kiss
I am saving for only you.

Higher

This is how it feels
when I see you walking toward me.

      My heart beats faster,
      The floor collapses.
      The ceiling flies away.

When you look into my eyes
my heart has wings
   and my soul is
reborn and baptized
by the fire in your eyes.

Then, slowly, I feel myself
melting Into your essence
   and I am sky high
as you touch my hand
   and take me higher.

Longer Than Forever

I love to look at you.
I love to touch you.
I love to be near you.
I simply love you
              totally,
          irrevocably
    in every way shape and form.

    For me
the sun does not
      rise in the east
      and set in the west.
It rises when you open your eyes
and sets when you lie down to rest.

    I could say and write
a million beautiful words for you
but the most important words
  I can ever say to you are:
  "I will always love you
    longer than forever."

Shine This Dream

   Your eyes find me
in the deep of the night
and the dark of my dream
    and I am comforted.

I feel you on every level
and I dream a sweeter dream
just knowing you are near,

        Flash your eyes.
        Mesmerize me.
        Radiate your electricity
    and magnetize me to your body.

Handcuff my heart to your soul
and shackle my kiss to your lips
    then shine this dream
      that it may last forever.

YOU

There are voices
and there are 'voices';
but none so sweet to my hearing
      as yours.

And there are faces,
many faces,
but none as deeply engraved
into my heart and soul
      as yours.

And then there is the touch;
"your touch" like no other ...

      Unforgettable.
        YOU.

Your Rhythm

When I lay in silence
alone in my room
      I think on you.

         I feel your rhythm
      inside my body and soul:
           above me,
          below me,
           inside me.

    As your essence surrounds me
       in complete satisfaction
    all else pales in comparison.

YOU Forever

In the vast and full effulgence
of creation and creativity,
every time I see you
I am more alive,
breathe deeper
and am more in synch with
the ever-turning wheel of destiny.

Life, death, and life.
Again and again.
Parallel and Concurrent.

For me ...
YOU forever.

We Have No Choice

Whatever it turns out to be
will be what it is meant to be.

    You, me,
  who we are
 and what we become
is subject to the universe
 and its inner workings
turning the wheel of fate.

    ALWAYS
  It is what it was.
  It is what it is.
It is what it will ever be.

All time is happening now
  in continuous overlap
    of fate..
  We can't outrun it.
It will always find us
and sew us together
  or rip us apart.

  In and out of time,
we are but the pawns
 of destiny's whims

We have no choice.

We have no choice.

Imagination's Reverie

Candice James served 2 terms (2010-2016) as Poet Laureate of New Westminster BC CANADA and was appointed Poet Laureate Emerita by order of City Council in November 2016. She is also a visual artist; a musician; a singer/songwriter; a workshop facilitator , book reviewer; and the author of 22 books of poetry. She is also co-author with Matthew Jose re the "Double Trouble "far out fantasy" poetry series Volumes 1 through 5". Her poetry has been translated in Arabic, Bengali, Farsi, Chinese, Italian and French and has appeared in a variety of international anthologies and magazines.

She is also Founder of Royal City Literary Arts Society; Poetic Justice; Poetry in the Park; Poetry New Westminster; RCLAS Singer Songwriters; Fred Cogswell Award for Excellence in Poetry and she is the recipient of the Bernie Legge Artist Cultural Award and Pandora's Collective Citizenship Award.

Candice's paintings and artwork have appeared in many magazines internationally including Duende (Goddard University of Fine Arts, Vermont); SurVision, (Ireland); The Arts and Entertainment Magazine (Hollywood); CQ International, (New York); and Wax, Poetry Art Magazine (Canada). Her songs have been recorded and released by many recording artists in North America and Europe.

For further info visit
www.silverbowpublishing.com
or
www.candicejames.com

www.ingramcontent.com/pod-product-compliance
Lightning Source LLC
Chambersburg PA
CBHW071025080526
44587CB00015B/2502